Women in Profile

Political Leaders

Janice Parker

Crabtree Publishing Company

Dedication

This series is dedicated to every woman who has followed her dreams and to every young girl who hopes to do the same. While overcoming great odds and often oppression, the remarkable women in this series have triumphed in their fields. Their dedication, hard work, and excellence can serve as an inspiration to all—young and old, male and female. Women in Profile is both an acknowledgment of and a tribute to these great women.

Project Manager
Lauri Seidlitz
Crabtree Editor
Virginia Mainprize
Copy Editors
Krista McLuskey
Leslie Strudwick
Design and Layout
Warren Clark

Published by Crabtree Publishing Company

350 Fifth Avenue, Suite 3308
New York, NY
USA 10018

360 York Road, R.R. 4
Niagara-on-the-Lake
Ontario, Canada
L0S 1J0

Copyright © 1998 WEIGL EDUCATIONAL PUBLISHERS LIMITED. All rights reserved. No part of this publication may be reproduced, stored in a retrieval system or be transmitted in any form or by any means, electronic, mechanical, photocopying, recording, or otherwise, without the prior written permission of Weigl Educational Publishers Limited.

Cataloging-in-Publication Data

Parker, Janice
    Political leaders / Janice Parker.
        p. cm. — (Women in profile)
    Includes bibliographical references and index.
    Summary: Describes the lives and political careers of such women as Corazon Aquino, Benazir Bhutto, Indira Gandhi, Golda Meir, Eva Peron, and Margaret Thatcher.
    ISBN 0-7787-0008-9 (RLB). — ISBN 0-7787-0030-5 (PB)
    1. Women presidents—Biography—Juvenile literature. 2. Women prime ministers—Biography—Juvenile literature. 3. Women in politics—Juvenile literature. [1. Women presidents. 2. Women prime ministers. 3. Presidents. 4. Prime ministers. 5. Women in politics. 6. Women—Biography.] I. Title. II. Series.
D839.5.P37 1998   97-53282
920.72—dc21   CIP
                                  AC

Photograph Credits
Every reasonable effort has been made to trace ownership and to obtain permission to reprint copyright material. The publishers would be pleased to have any errors or omissions brought to their attention so that they may be corrected in subsequent printings.
Archive Photos: cover, pages 12, 30, 32, 33; Canapress Photo Service: page 11; Globe Photos: pages 13 (Arnaud Fevrier), 25 (Crispian Woodgate-Manité), 34 (George G. Grechowicz), 40 (Steve Finn), 44 (Diego Goldberg), 10, 16, 18, 19, 20, 22, 24, 26, 29; Embassy of the Republic of Lithuania: page 45; Photofest: pages 21, 31, 37, 38; Reuters/Corbis-Bettmann: pages 9 (Romeo Ranoco), 6, 8, 17; Rosana Solorzano: page 42; Topham Picture Point: pages 14, 36, 39, 41; United States Consulate: page 43; UPI/Corbis-Bettmann: pages 23, 27; Linda Weigl: page 35.

Contents

Political Leaders

W ho comes to mind when you think about a political leader? Chances are good that you think of a man. Until the twentieth century, very few women had led their countries. However, women have always been leaders. Throughout history, women from different cultures and continents have led their families and communities. Now they are leading their countries, too.

Becoming a successful political leader means overcoming many challenges. Some challenges are faced by anyone, man or woman, who tries to achieve political success. Obstacles may include living in a country with widespread poverty, a poorly educated population, or a history of political unrest and war. Other obstacles are especially difficult for women. Some countries limit women's education and career choices because of religious or cultural beliefs. The women in this book have overcome many challenges to bring about change in their countries.

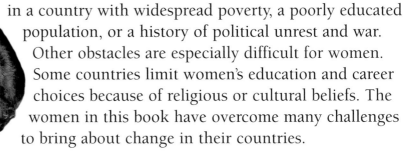

The political leaders in this volume were chosen from a long list of great women. They are not remarkable simply because they are women. Some of these women may have been "the first woman to...," but their accomplishments are so great that they would be notable even if they were "the hundredth woman to...."

Political Leaders profiles the stories of outstanding women leaders. Presidents, prime ministers, and even a few first ladies, these women come from different continents, cultures, religions, economic situations, and time periods. What makes them stand out is their influence on the political events of their countries. The first ladies profiled here were not elected to political office, but they used their positions as political leaders to work for the people of their countries. This book is a tribute to a wide range of outstanding women. In addition to the six major profiles, it includes brief descriptions of other leaders you may wish to investigate further.

Read about these women's lives, their accomplishments, and their strength in the face of trouble. Many of these women did not have role models. However, they may be role models for you.

"My political strength rests on popular support ... in people power and the nonviolent approach."

Corazon Aquino
President of the Philippines

Early Years

Corazon grew up in a large, wealthy, and politically active family. She started school when she was three. She was eight when the Japanese invaded the Philippines during World War II. Corazon's home and school were damaged during the war. Much of her country was destroyed, and a million Filipinos were killed. Corazon's parents decided to move their family to the United States.

When her parents returned to the Philippines after a year, Corazon stayed in the United States to attend high school and college. She was a quiet young woman and an excellent student. In 1953, Corazon returned to the Philippines to study law.

While Corazon was at university, she met a childhood friend, Benigno Aquino, a journalist who was also studying law. The two soon fell in love, and in 1954, they married. They moved to a large sugar and rice plantation near Benigno's hometown.

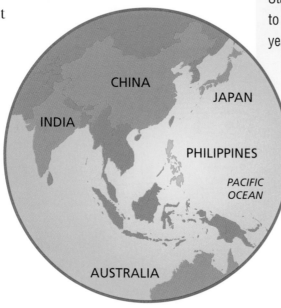

BACKGROUNDER

A Troubled Past

Throughout its history, the Philippines has been ruled by many nations. Its location makes it a **strategic** post for countries at war in the area. From the sixteenth century to the twentieth century, Spain ruled the Philippines. After the Spanish-American War in 1901, the United States controlled it. In 1941, the Japanese invaded the Philippines. The United States **surrendered** the islands to the Japanese the following year. In 1944, the United States took control of the area again. Then in 1946, the Philippines gained **independence** from foreign rule.

BACKGROUNDER

Ferdinand Marcos

In 1965, Ferdinand Marcos became president of the Philippines. At first, Ferdinand was very popular. He built new roads and schools and improved agriculture. The country needed this development. It had not yet fully recovered from the destruction of World War II. By the late 1960s, many people were unhappy with Ferdinand's government. They believed Ferdinand was helping himself more than his country. People such as Benigno wanted the Philippines to be a **democracy** where people could vote for their leaders. Ferdinand began to lose control of the country, so in 1972, he declared martial law. This meant that the country became a **dictatorship**, and he gained enormous power.

Developing Skills

W hen Benigno ran in an **election** for mayor of their town, Corazon also became involved in politics. Soon, she had no private life. People dropped by her home at all hours, and she worked hard on her husband's campaign.

Benigno was elected mayor and later governor. The role of the wife of a politician was new to Corazon. For inspiration, she turned to her mother-in-law, Dona Aurora, who had been married to a politician for many years. From Dona Aurora, Corazon learned how to talk to strangers. She also learned the importance of speaking to people in their own language.

Benigno worked long days, and Corazon was often alone while she raised her five children. Although she always supported her husband's career, she was lonely without him.

In 1972, the president, Ferdinand Marcos, declared himself dictator of the Philippines. He took away people's civil rights and freedoms and jailed those who disagreed with his views. Benigno was a political enemy of the president and was sent to prison. He was kept there for more than seven years.

Corazon first became a public figure when her husband ran for mayor.

Although Corazon was terrified, she realized that she would have to stay strong for the sake of her husband and children. She acted as Benigno's messenger and represented him in public. During this time, she learned much about politics.

One day, Benigno disappeared from jail. The police returned his clothing and eyeglasses to Corazon. Not knowing if her husband was dead or alive, she joined hundreds of other women outside the prison. They were all waiting to find out if their loved ones were still alive. Eventually, Benigno was found. He had been placed in solitary confinement.

The United States, which supported Ferdinand, pressured him to hold an election. Benigno decided to oppose Ferdinand and run in the election from his jail cell. Corazon became his campaign manager. She held news conferences and spread Benigno's message to the people. However, only Ferdinand and those who agreed with his views were elected. After Benigno suffered a serious heart attack in 1980, he was allowed to travel to the United States for a heart operation. He, Corazon, and their family were told not to return to the Philippines.

Corazon never thought that she would become a politician. She learned how to be a good leader through her own sense of justice and by helping her husband with his political career.

"Twenty years of corruption, greed, waste, and near-despair have finally ended. They were ended by a revolution of peace, prayers, rosaries, radios and, above all, human courage."

Accomplishments

The 1996 Fulbright Prize was awarded to Corazon for her courage, integrity, and commitment to restoring democracy to the Philippines.

Corazon and her family led a quiet life in the United States. Benigno had a good job at the Harvard Center for International Affairs. However, he still hoped to find a way to help his country. In 1983, Benigno decided to return to the Philippines. Corazon wanted him to stay with their family in the United States where they were safe, but she knew that it was important for him to return. When Benigno arrived at the Philippines airport, he was **assassinated**.

In shock, Corazon returned with her family to the Philippines to bury her husband. Once again, she stepped into the public eye. She demanded justice for Benigno's death and for all of the other people who had been killed for their political beliefs. She decided to work against Ferdinand's government. Soon, Corazon became a symbol for her country's fight for freedom.

BACKGROUNDER

Benigno's Assassination

Although Corazon and Benigno were safe in the United States, Benigno wanted to return to his country to fight Ferdinand's government. Imelda Marcos, Ferdinand's wife, had warned Benigno that it would be dangerous to return to the Philippines. Benigno knew that someone might try to kill him, but he felt it was his duty to help his country. On his trip back, he phoned Corazon and wrote a letter to each of his children. When Benigno arrived in the Philippines, he was shot and killed as he left the airplane. Although the government said that a criminal had killed him, most people thought that Ferdinand had hired someone to assassinate Benigno.

Corazon gave speeches against Ferdinand's government. In 1985, she decided to run against him in the next election. Corazon traveled all over the country to talk to people. Unlike many politicians, she wrote most of her own speeches. She urged people to end Ferdinand's rule by voting against him.

When all of the votes were counted after the election, the results were not made public for several days. Ferdinand Marcos tried to hide the fact that Corazon had won the election. Thousands of people went into the streets of Manila, the Philippine capital, to protest against Ferdinand and his government. Eventually, the United States forced Ferdinand and his wife to leave the Philippines. Corazon became president of the country.

Corazon had to deal with many problems. The economy was poor, and Ferdinand's supporters plotted to take over her government. Corazon tried to treat everyone fairly, even those who did not want her to be in power. She believed that problems could be resolved peacefully. In 1987, however, a violent attempt by rebels to take over the government was almost successful. Many innocent people were killed.

Corazon ruled the Philippines until 1992 when she stepped down as president. She had been in power during six of the most difficult years for her country. Because of Corazon, democracy returned to the Philippines, and people could vote for their political leaders.

"Women are less liable to resort to violence than men."

Quick Notes

- **Corazon's Catholic faith is very important to her.**

- **During Benigno's imprisonment, Corazon's family nicknamed her "wonder woman" and "woman of steel." This was because of the strength she showed during that difficult time.**

- **The color yellow, which stands for love and support, came to represent Corazon's fight for freedom for the Philippines. She often wore yellow, and her supporters handed out yellow posters and t-shirts. Corazon wore a yellow dress when she took her oath as president.**

Key Events

1976 Elected president of the Oxford Debating Club, the first woman and first non-British person to win the honor

1977 Graduates from Oxford University

1978 Publishes the book *Foreign Policy in Perspective*

1987 Marries Asif Ali Zardari

1988 Is the first woman elected prime minister of Pakistan

1988 Gives birth to a son two months after winning the election

1988 Wins Bruno Kreisty Human Rights Award

1988 Publishes the book *Daughter of Destiny*

1990 Gives birth to a daughter

1990 Removed from power by the president

1993 Re-elected prime minister

1996 Removed from power by the president

1997 Wins a seat in government, but her party loses the election

"My politics are a commitment to freedom and the meaning of life."

Benazir Bhutto

Prime Minister of Pakistan

Early Years

Benazir grew up in a wealthy and modern family. Her father, Ali Bhutto, believed that men and women were equals. Benazir's mother, Nusrat, was well educated. This was unusual in Pakistan in the 1950s. Many people believed that women did not need an education. They thought that husbands should make all the important decisions.

The Bhutto family was an exception. Benazir started nursery school when she was three years old. She went to a private school two years later. Benazir studied many subjects, including English and mathematics. She liked to play soccer, field hockey, and volleyball.

Encouraged by her father, Benazir read as much as she could. She especially liked history books about leaders such as Napoleon and Abraham Lincoln, and books about the history of India and **Islam**.

When she was sixteen, Benazir went to study at Radcliffe College in Cambridge, Massachusetts. She was frightened to leave Pakistan but was excited to travel to the United States.

BACKGROUNDER

Muslim Women and the Veil

The *burqa* is a heavy, dark garment that **Muslim** women use to cover their body and face in public and when strange men are in the room. Benazir's mother refused to wear a *burqa*. Benazir's parents decided that she did not have to wear one either.

Developing Skills

Benazir, who had always been shy, gained confidence at Radcliffe. She graduated with honors a few days before her twentieth birthday.

From there, she went to study politics and economics at Oxford University in England. She joined the Oxford Union **Debating** Society. Benazir loved the excitement of debating. Her first speech went so well that her fellow students voted 345 to 2 to support her opinion. The debating club gave her the chance to practice the skills she would need when she entered politics. Benazir's three years at Oxford went by quickly. She did well in her studies and made many friends.

Meanwhile, back in Pakistan, the political situation was changing. Benazir's father disagreed with how the Pakistani government was run. In 1967, Ali formed his own **political party**, the Pakistan People's Party (PPP).

Benazir's years at university gave her confidence for her public life.

The Pakistani president was angered by the new party and put Ali in jail. In 1970, Pakistan held its first free **election** in many years, and Ali Bhutto was elected prime minister.

Benazir followed political events in Pakistan and was eager to return home to work for her country and spend time with her family. Her father, however, insisted that Benazir remain at Oxford for one more year to study international law and **diplomacy**. During that year, Benazir was elected the first woman president of the Oxford Union Debating Society.

Within days of returning to Pakistan in 1977, Benazir began working for her father. Her first job was sorting files in his office. She was very eager and wanted to learn all she could about politics.

BACKGROUNDER

The Creation of Pakistan

In the 1940s, India was trying to get **independence** from Britain. The two major religious groups in India, the Hindus and the Muslims, had formed separate political parties—the Indian National Congress and the Muslim League. The Muslim League believed the Hindus would have too much power when India gained independence from Britain. They wanted to have their own nation. After years of riots during the 1940s, Britain and the Hindu leaders finally agreed to divide the country. In 1947, India and Pakistan became independent countries. Pakistan included two areas on each side of India. Most Indian Muslims moved to East and West Pakistan, while most Hindus stayed in India. After a civil war in 1971, East Pakistan became the separate nation of Bangladesh.

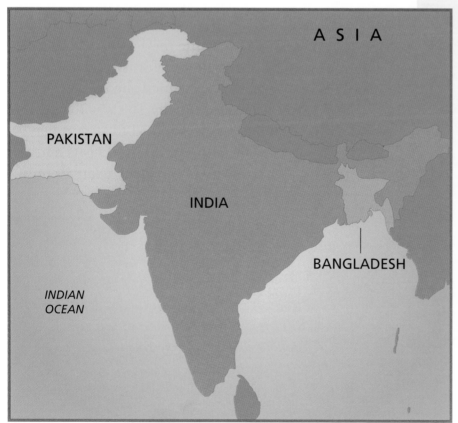

ASIA

PAKISTAN

INDIA

BANGLADESH

INDIAN OCEAN

Quick Notes

- Benazir's second name, Mohatarma, means "without equal" or "without comparison."

- Benazir's father nicknamed her "Pinkie" because she was so rosy and fair as a child.

- Benazir was going to study psychology at Radcliffe until she discovered that she might have to do experiments on animals. Her love of animals helped her decide to study politics instead.

Accomplishments

Everything changed for Benazir and her family in July 1977. Military leaders took over the government and placed Ali under arrest. He was falsely accused of murder. He was jailed and sentenced to death. Benazir and her mother were told not to leave their home. Benazir did everything she could to free her father. It was no use. Ali was executed in April 1979.

Benazir decided to carry on her father's political work by becoming the leader of the PPP, the political party her father had started. Other party members accepted Benazir because of their deep respect for her father. After becoming party leader, Benazir was often followed by secret police and was arrested several times by the military government.

In 1981, Benazir was imprisoned for several months. Her jail cell was small and cold. She was given little food and began to lose weight. Her only relief was receiving one newspaper a day, which she read over and over again. Eventually, she was released. However, she was forced to stay in her own home and was allowed visits and telephone calls from close relatives only.

"I would like Pakistan to be at peace with its neighbors. I would like it to be stable and independent. I would like Pakistan to emerge out of the darkness of illiteracy…. I would like to see equal opportunities for men and women."

Benazir had suffered from a serious ear infection for a long time. Her doctor said she needed special treatment in Europe. Finally, in 1984, the government allowed her to go to Switzerland for an operation. Later, she traveled to the United States and Europe, speaking publicly against the military government in Pakistan. She appealed to other nations for help.

In 1986, Benazir returned to Pakistan. She was elected prime minister in 1988. Benazir then faced the huge task of improving conditions in her country. She wanted to make Pakistan a **democracy**, with fair elections.

Benazir's time as leader of her country has been difficult. She has been removed as prime minister twice because of disagreements with Pakistan's president. In February 1997, Pakistan held elections. Although Benazir's party did poorly, she was elected again to serve in the government.

In 1989, Benazir delivered the Commencement Address at Howard University after receiving an honorary degree.

BACKGROUNDER

Problems in Pakistan

Benazir faced many challenges as prime minister of Pakistan. The military was very powerful and was often **corrupt**. The former prime minister had used the extreme laws of Islam to support his policies. Women had few rights and were often sent to prison for little or no reason. Drugs were easy to get in Pakistan. Farmers could earn more money growing poppies (used to make heroin) than they could growing food crops. Pakistan also has a serious population problem. The nation's population grew from 50 million in 1960 to 130 million in 1996. Sometimes there was not enough food for everyone. Benazir tried to combat hunger by encouraging farmers to grow food crops that can earn as much money as poppies. She is also working hard to improve education and give more rights to women.

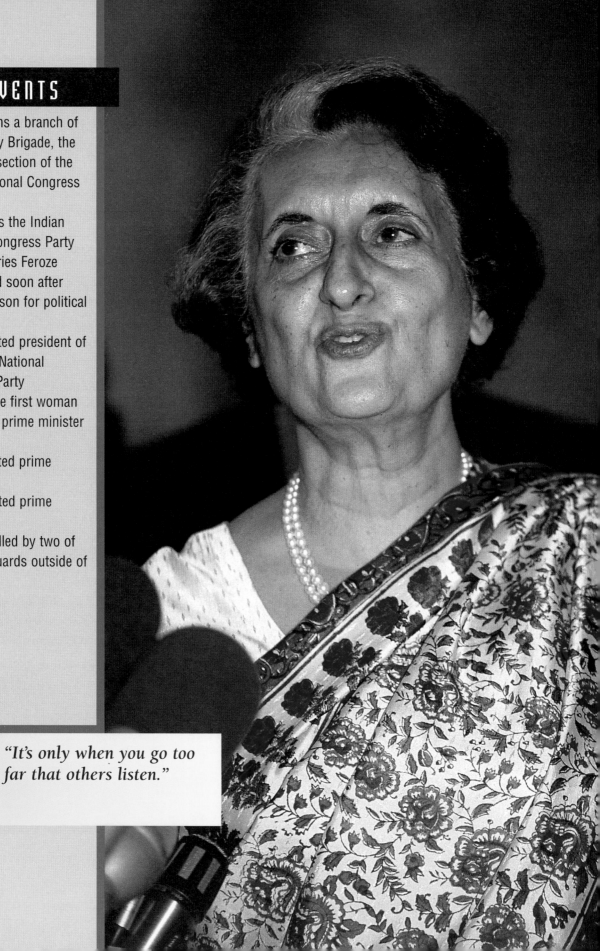

"It's only when you go too far that others listen."

Indira Gandhi

Prime Minister of India

Early Years

When Indira was born in 1917, her family lived in a huge house with a pool, tennis courts, and many servants. When Indira was three years old, the Indian freedom movement changed her life.

At that time, Indira's father, Jawaharlal Nehru, became a strong supporter of Indian leader Mohandas Gandhi. Gandhi wanted India to be free from British rule. He also believed that people should live a simple life. Under Gandhi's influence, Indira's family burned all of their British possessions, including one of Indira's favorite dolls. They began wearing Indian dress instead of Western clothing. Their family home became a meeting place for members of the Indian National Congress Party (INC), an organization of people who wanted Indian **independence** from Britain.

Indira's childhood was lonely and difficult. Her father and mother and other members of her family were often imprisoned for their political beliefs. Indira was sometimes sent to live with relatives. At times, Indira pretended that her dolls were Indian freedom fighters or British soldiers.

BACKGROUNDER

Mohandas Gandhi

Mohandas Gandhi was a close friend of Indira's family. Gandhi was called Mahatma, which means "great soul." He was a member of the Indian National Congress Party. Gandhi preached nonviolence and **tolerance** of all people and religions.

Indira Gandhi with her parents in 1918.

BACKGROUNDER

Religion and the Caste System in India

There are many religious groups in India, including Buddhists, Christians, Hindus, Jains, Muslims, and Sikhs. About eighty-three percent of Indian people are Hindu. Hindus are divided into different social groups, called castes. There are high castes and low castes. Each caste has strict rules and rituals. A person is born into a caste and cannot leave it. Indira's family was Brahmin, the highest caste.

Developing Skills

By the time she was twelve, Indira was doing more than playing politics. She formed the Monkey Brigade, a branch of the children's section of the Congress Party. They delivered secret messages, ran errands, and even spied on police stations.

Indira's mother suffered from tuberculosis, a lung disease, and went to Switzerland to recover. Indira traveled with her and spent two years in Swiss schools. In 1936, Indira's mother died, and her father was elected president of the INC Party. Indira joined the party when she was twenty.

When she was twenty-four, Indira decided to marry Feroze Gandhi, a journalist and family friend. Indira's father objected to the marriage at first. Feroze's family was from a different social class and religion than Indira's family. As well, Hindu marriages are usually arranged by the parents. Indira insisted that she would marry Feroze, so finally Indira's father allowed the wedding to take place.

Soon after her marriage, Indira was sent to jail by the British for eight months because of her support for the INC Party. Her new husband also ended up in prison. Indira spent her twenty-fifth birthday in jail.

"In India, women have never been in hostile competition with men—even in the most distant past, every time a woman emerged as a leader, perhaps as a queen, people accepted her."

When they were released, the couple moved to a small house, and Indira seemed ready to settle into her role as wife. Within two years she had two sons, Rajiv and Sanjay.

After World War II ended, India became independent from Britain. In the 1947 **elections**, Indira's father became the first prime minister of independent India. Indira became an unofficial first lady for her father. Although Indira was shy in social situations, she believed she had to help her father.

In her new role, Indira was often separated from Feroze. Eventually, Indira and her two sons moved in with her father, while Feroze moved into his own house. The two rarely saw each other, although they never divorced.

Indira learned about politics from watching and traveling with her father. She met other world leaders and went to important meetings. In 1959, she became president of the INC Party, but after one year, she left the position so that she could help her father. By this time, she was a confident politician.

When Indira's father died of a heart attack in 1964, many thought that Indira's career in politics was over. The new prime minister gave her only a minor position in the government. Some people believed that Indira had no influence without her father's support. They underestimated her strength and determination.

In 1965, Indira visited a memorial exhibit to her father with famous Americans such as Jacqueline Kennedy.

Quick Notes

- Indira's second name, Priyadarshini, means "dear to behold" or "beautiful to behold."

- Indira's aunt, Vijaya Lakshmi Pandit, was the first woman president of the United Nations.

- Indira's father sent her a series of letters from jail outlining important events in world history. These letters were later published in a book called *Freedom's Daughter*.

"I do not regard myself as a woman. I am a person with a job to do."

Accomplishments

During India's war with Pakistan in 1965, Indira showed true courage. She visited dangerous areas close to the India-Pakistan borders. She gave speeches to help keep up the **morale** of the soldiers.

When the prime minister of India died suddenly of a heart attack in 1966, the INC Party chose Indira to take his place. They thought that they would be able to control her.

Indira became the youngest and the first female prime minister in India's history. When asked how she felt about her responsibilities, she told reporters that it "was just another job I have to do." India had many problems. Crops had been destroyed by bad weather, and wars had been expensive. Indira was not afraid of the challenge. She had a great deal of practice talking to the Indian people and dealing with other countries.

In the 1967 elections, Indira traveled around India giving speeches and became well known throughout the country. Indira was never afraid of people who disapproved of her. During one of her speeches, someone in the audience threw a large stone at her that broke her nose. Despite the pain, Indira refused to leave. She held a cloth to her bloody nose and finished her speech. She continued her speaking tour with bandages on her face. Her calm behavior impressed many of her country's people.

Indira was not popular with everyone in her party. Many older party members did not agree with her ideas. Eventually, the party split into two groups: one that supported Indira and another that did not.

During Indira's years in power, India had economic problems that many people blamed on her. Some government officials tried to have her arrested and put in jail. At one point, Indira called a state of emergency. Many of her opponents were put into prison, and freedoms were limited. By doing this, Indira hung on to her power.

Indira and her party lost the 1977 election. Indira refused to give up. She continued to make speeches and meet people around the country. Only thirty-three months later, she again became prime minister. Indira led India until 1984, when she was **assassinated**.

Indira walks in her garden with her son Rajiv. Within hours of her death, Rajiv was named prime minister of India.

Backgrounder

The Assassination

Indira was assassinated outside her office by two trusted Sikh bodyguards. Sikhs have their own religion and live in a part of India called the Punjab. Some Sikhs wanted the Punjab to be a separate nation. In 1984, they took over a Sikh temple and threatened to **terrorize** India until their demands were met. When they would not leave the temple peacefully, Indira sent in the army. Over six hundred people were killed, including an important Sikh leader. To protest these killings, Indira's bodyguards shot her.

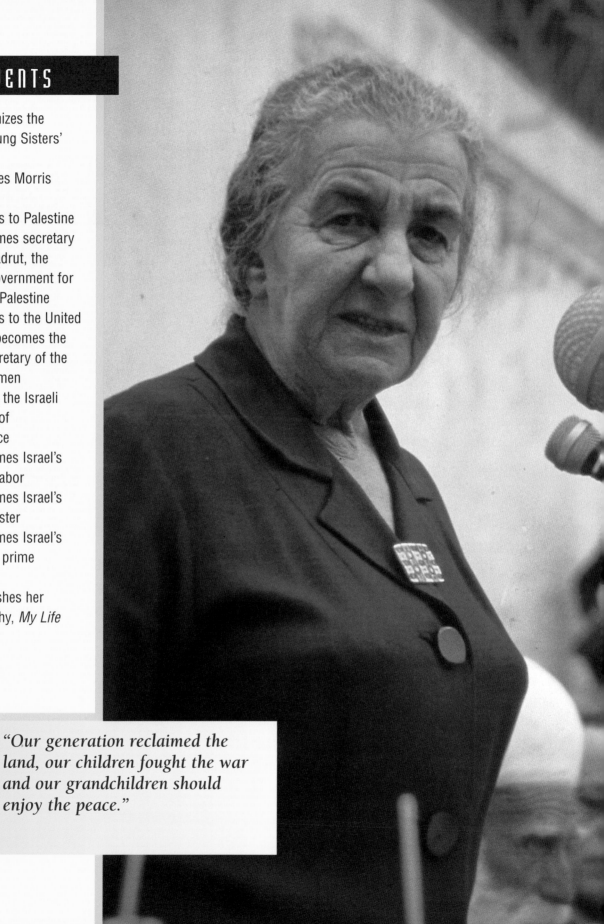

"Our generation reclaimed the land, our children fought the war and our grandchildren should enjoy the peace."

Golda Meir

Prime Minister of Israel

Early Years

Golda was born in Russia, the third daughter of a Jewish family. Jews were discriminated against and **persecuted** by other Russians. Golda's earliest memory was of her family boarding up their home to protect themselves from a group of Russian soldiers who were robbing and killing Jews. Although Golda's father was a talented cabinetmaker, he was usually underpaid or not paid at all. When Golda was five, her father went to the United States to try to earn more money.

In 1906, Golda's father asked the family to join him in America. They knew that they would never return to their friends and relatives in Russia. The voyage to the United States was difficult and took more than a month. Golda's mother and two sisters were seasick. Their luggage was stolen, and they were given little food on the ship.

Golda was glad to reach her new home in Milwaukee, Wisconsin. She was thrilled with the size of their apartment, her new clothes, and especially with school. Golda was a good student. When she was ten, she organized the America Young Sisters' Society, a group that bought schoolbooks for children who could not afford them.

BACKGROUNDER

Russian Jews

Life was hard for Russian Jews at the turn of the century. Although they paid taxes and served in the army like all other Russians, they were treated like second-class citizens. Most Jews lived in poverty. Two or three families often shared one small, dark house. Sometimes, soldiers came into a Jewish village and burned the houses and killed all the people.

After facing persecution as a child in Russia, Golda began dreaming of a homeland for Jewish people.

Developing Skills

When Golda was fourteen, her parents asked her to drop out of school and marry a much older man. They thought that there was no need for girls to have an education. Golda wanted to stay in school, so she ran away to live with her older, married sister. When she was sixteen, Golda returned to live with her parents. She became active in a Zionist group. Zionism was the movement to establish a Jewish homeland in Palestine, an area in the Middle East. Golda traveled and gave speeches for the right of Jewish people to have a state of their own.

Golda's work for the Histadrut prepared her for her later job as leader of her country.

In 1917, Golda married. She and her husband, Morris, decided to move to Palestine. They lived and worked on a kibbutz, a large farm where people own the land and farm together. The couple later moved to Jerusalem, the capital of Palestine, and had two children. Golda worked for the Histadrut, the unofficial government for the Jews in Palestine. Her new job required Golda to go on speaking tours and set up training courses for Jewish girls who came to Palestine to work on the land. She was often separated from her husband and children.

In 1932, Golda and her family moved back to the United States for two years so that her daughter could be treated for kidney disease. Golda became the national secretary of the Pioneer Women, a group that tried to spread the Zionist message among American women.

In 1938, Golda went to an international conference on how countries could help Jews wanting to escape Hitler's persecution in Germany before World War II. Golda was stunned when not one country offered to help. During World War II, Hitler and the Nazis killed more than six million Jews—over two-thirds of the Jews in Europe.

In 1940, Golda became the head of the political department of the Histadrut. She was the **liaison** between Britain and the Jewish people in Palestine. After the war, Golda continued to fight for a Jewish state.

"Anybody who believes in something without reservation, believes that this thing is right and should be, has the stamina to meet obstacles and overcome them ... but I was never so naive or foolish as to think that if you merely believe in something it happens. You must struggle for it."

Backgrounder

Palestine

Until almost 2,000 years ago, most of the area that was called Palestine was the homeland of the Jewish people. Later, this part of the Middle East was ruled by many different groups, including Persians, Romans, Turks, and following World War I, the British. In the Balfour Declaration of 1920, Britain supported the idea of creating a Jewish homeland in Palestine. However, Arabs, who had also lived in the area for centuries, opposed the declaration. As a result, in 1939, just before World War II, the British decided to limit the number of Jews allowed into Palestine. The British stopped a ship full of Jewish refugees from landing in Palestine. In protest, the passengers and several Jewish leaders, including Golda, went on a **hunger strike**. They finally convinced the British to allow the ship to land and the refugees to leave the ship.

BACKGROUNDER

The State of Israel

In 1948, part of Palestine became the state of Israel. It was the first time in 2,000 years that the Jewish people had a homeland of their own. Jewish survivors of Hitler's Holocaust, and Jews from around the world, began to pour into Israel. Israel's Arab neighbors were unhappy with the creation of the Jewish state and often threatened Israel with war.

Accomplishments

By 1947, the problems between the Jews and the Arabs in Palestine had increased. Britain turned to the **United Nations** (U.N.) for help. The U.N. decided to divide Palestine into two parts: a Jewish state (Israel) and an Arab state (Transjordan). As part of the Jewish National Council, Golda signed the new Israeli Declaration of **Independence** on May 15, 1948. That very day, armies from several neighboring Arab countries attacked Israel to protest the creation of the state of Israel.

Golda's first task was to raise money to help Israel's army. She went to the United States where she raised a great deal of money. Then she went to the Soviet Union, representing her country there as Israel's ambassador. Israel held its first **elections** in 1949. Golda was elected to the Knesset, Israel's Parliament, and became the minister of labor. She made housing and job creation her most important work. She began a program to build thirty thousand new housing units. She also worked to create laws to increase the rights of women.

TURKEY

MEDITERRANEAN SEA

LEBANON   SYRIA

ISRAEL

JORDAN

EGYPT

SAUDI
ARABIA

When another war with the Arab states threatened Israel in 1956, Golda was asked to become foreign minister. The prime minister insisted that she change her last name, Meyerson, to a Hebrew name, Meir. When asked what it felt like to be the first woman foreign minister of Israel, Golda replied, "I don't know, I was never a man minister."

In 1966, Golda hoped to retire so that she would have time to read, cook, and spend time with her grandchildren. However, Israel needed her, and she became the secretary-general of the United Labor Party. Another Arab-Israeli war broke out in 1967, and the Arabs were quickly defeated. Two years later, the prime minister died of a heart attack. In 1969, Golda was elected prime minister.

In 1973, Arab armies suddenly attacked Israel from all sides. Some people blamed Golda for having allowed Arab troops to build up on Israel's borders. Although the Arab armies were pushed back, Golda resigned as prime minister. She was seventy-five years old and suffering from cancer. Today, Golda is remembered as one of Israel's most important political figures.

Quick Notes

- **Golda was nicknamed Goldie by her family.**

- **Golda and her doctors kept her cancer a secret for more than fifteen years. During those years, Golda refused to let the disease prevent her from working.**

Golda spoke to the media during the fourth Arab-Israeli war which broke out in October 1973.

KEY EVENTS

1934 Moves to Buenos Aires to become an actor

1942 Gets her own radio show

1946 Marries Juan Perón

1946 Becomes first lady when Juan is elected president

1947 Visits Spain and other European countries as a representative of Argentina

1948 Gets Argentinian women the right to vote in elections. Given the title "Spiritual Mother of all Argentinian children"

1951 Publishes her autobiography, *La razón de mi vida* (*My Life's Work*)

1952 Dies of cancer

Eva Perón

First Lady of Argentina

Early Years

The child of an unwed mother, Eva spent her early years in poverty. She and her family were treated unkindly by the people in the small Argentinian town where they lived. When Eva was seven, her father died. Eva's family was not allowed to attend his funeral.

When Eva was twelve, her family moved to a bigger town where they hoped life would be better. Eva dreamed of a career as an actor. At fifteen, she convinced a well-known tango singer to let her travel with his company to Buenos Aires, Argentina's capital city.

Eva soon learned that life was as difficult in the city as it was in smaller towns. She was alone, knew no one, and had no work experience. Yet she was determined to succeed. Eva got small parts acting in radio plays. Soon, she began to make money, and she became a celebrity.

BACKGROUNDER

Democracy versus Dictatorship

In 1853, Argentina created a **constitution** similar to that of the United States. The country became a **democracy** in which the people elected their leaders. In the late 1920s, the Great Depression started to ruin Argentina's economy. Many people blamed the government for their problems. In 1930, army leaders removed the elected president from office. Since then, Argentina has often been ruled by a military **dictatorship** in which one person or a small group of people have complete control over the country.

Eva's popularity took off when she started work for a radio show called "Famous Women." Each week she was heard across the country playing the roles of women such as Catherine the Great and Sarah Bernhardt.

Developing Skills

In 1944, Eva met Colonel Juan Domingo Perón, a politician. They fell in love immediately. With Juan's help, Eva began to get better parts on the radio. She even landed some film roles and was also given a small job in the government. Juan became vice-president. Soon after, he was arrested by his enemies in the government. They had decided to hold an **election** and were afraid that Juan might win and become too powerful.

"My greatest satisfaction … would be to offer my hand to all those who carry inside them the flame of faith in something or in someone and in those who harbor a hope."

Life without Juan was not easy for Eva. Once, while she was riding in a taxi, a street gang recognized her as Juan's girlfriend. They pulled her out of the car and beat her. At the same time, many of Juan's supporters called for his release. After a general strike by workers, Juan was freed. He returned to Buenos Aires and married Eva five days later. With Eva's help, he began his campaign to become president. Never before had the wife of a candidate toured with him during a presidential campaign. Soon, Eva became as popular as her husband. The crowds loved her, although many in the upper classes resented her popularity and influence. In 1946, Juan was elected president of Argentina.

Juan and Eva in June 1952.

As wife of the president, Eva became the first lady of Argentina. She worked hard. She often gave speeches for Juan. Many people said she was one of the best speakers in Argentina. She worked eighteen-hour days and headed the Ministry of Labor and Welfare. However, some people did not think Juan should have given his wife a government job. They were also angry that Eva had given many of her friends and relatives positions in the government. She was accused of spending too much government money on herself. Some reports claimed that in 207 days, she had worn 306 different dresses. Some people said that a plane had been sent to Paris so that a gown could be flown back for Eva.

In response to the criticism, Eva changed her image. She wore her hair in a simple style and chose simpler and less expensive clothes. She also decided to help Argentina's poor by founding the Eva Perón Foundation to raise money for social programs.

BACKGROUNDER

The First Lady

Although the position of first lady does not have official power in Argentina, Eva considered her role to be very important. Many people were angry that a radio and film actor had so much power. However, Eva forced people to take her seriously through her hard work helping the people of her country improve their lives.

Eva was adored by many Argentinians. To some, her life represented the dream of moving from poverty to wealth and success.

BACKGROUNDER

The Perón Legacy

Government spending while Juan was president left Argentina nearly **bankrupt**. Juan also suspended several **civil rights** while in office, such as freedom of speech and freedom of the press. In 1955, military leaders overthrew Juan's government. Juan became president again in 1973. He died the following year.

Accomplishments

The Argentinian people loved Eva. She began to give her own speeches instead of Juan's. She refused to say things that just echoed her husband's words. Eva put most of her energy into helping the Argentinian people. She built houses for the poor, hospitals and homes for the elderly, and she worked to make drinking water safe.

Many of her programs helped working-class children. Eva started a vacation camp for low-income children. She gave socks and shoes to young soccer players. She also built a special children's park that was both educational and fun. In 1948, she was given the title "Spiritual Mother of all Argentinian Children."

Eva's popularity grew with each of her speeches. At one appearance in Tucuman, nine people were killed in the rush of people trying to see Eva.

Eva also fought for women's rights. Her work helped Argentinian women get the right to vote in elections. Eva became a popular figure, especially with working people. Eva even sent money to less fortunate countries. However, she spent so much money that some people accused her of making the government bankrupt.

By 1950, Eva's energy started to fade. She was often in pain and sometimes fainted in public. She discovered that she had cancer and had an operation early in the year. Her health improved, and she decided to run for vice-president in 1951. However, many military leaders were afraid that Eva might become president one day, so they stopped her from running.

Soon after, Eva's cancer worsened. She spent most of her time in bed, and the truth about her health was hidden from the Argentinian people. Eva wrote her **autobiography**, *La razón de mi vida* (*My Life's Work*), which quickly became a bestseller. The book was made required reading for all schoolchildren in Argentina.

The few times that Eva did appear in public, she was so weak that her husband had to support her. Eva died of cancer in 1952 at the age of thirty-three. After her death, forty thousand appeals were sent to the Roman Catholic Church asking that she be made a saint.

Quick notes

- Eva was also known as Evita.

- Eva's embalmed body mysteriously disappeared in 1955. It was returned sixteen years later.

- In 1977, Tim Rice and Andrew Lloyd Webber wrote the musical *Evita* about Eva's life.

Eva was buried in her father's family plot in Buenos Aires. Visitors still leave flowers at the site.

"There's no point in getting too sensitive in politics."

Margaret Thatcher

Prime Minister of the United Kingdom

Early Years

Margaret's family had little money when she was a child growing up in England. Although she lived in a house without indoor plumbing or hot water, her father insisted that his children receive a good education. Margaret and her sister read newspapers, discussed current issues, and studied hard. They were not allowed to go to dances and had to attend church meetings several times a week. In high school, Margaret joined a **debating** club and took speech lessons.

Margaret became interested in politics when she was just a young girl. Her father was a part-time justice of the peace, and she often went with him to the courthouse. She was fascinated by what happened in the courtroom. However, Margaret decided to study chemistry because a teacher told her there were no jobs for women in law. When she was seventeen, Margaret went to Oxford University. Although she majored in chemistry, she remained interested in law and politics. She became president of the Oxford Union Conservative Association, a political group. When Margaret graduated, she found a job as a chemist, and she became involved with the Conservative Party.

BACKGROUNDER

World War II in Great Britain

Margaret was fourteen when World War II began. Her home town of Grantham had a big weapons industry, so it was often the target for German bombers. The Thatcher family hid under the dining room table during these air raids.

As a young woman, Margaret worked for the Conservative Party.

Margaret's husband, Denis Thatcher, supported her in her political goals.

Developing Skills

I n 1950, Margaret decided to run in the next **election** for a seat in Parliament. She lost. One year later, Margaret married Denis Thatcher. She decided to follow her dream and study law. Just two months after giving birth to twins, she wrote her law exams.

Although Margaret still wanted to be elected to Parliament, the Conservative Party turned her down because she had two young children. Margaret continued to practice law until her children went to school. Then, in 1959, she ran for and won a seat in Parliament. She was the youngest woman to be elected.

The Conservative Party leader, Edward Heath, was impressed by Margaret's abilities. When the Conservatives won the election in 1970, Margaret became secretary of education. One of her first decisions upset many people. The government wanted to save money, so Margaret stopped a program that gave free milk to schoolchildren. Many fellow politicians also disliked her. They thought she was too ambitious and cold. However, with hard work and other, more popular, decisions, such as giving money to rebuild schools, Margaret gained public respect.

Margaret surprised many people when she was elected leader of the Conservative Party in 1975.

When Margaret decided that she wanted to become prime minister, she worked hard to develop an image she felt suited a prime minister. She took lessons to improve her speaking voice. She had little experience in foreign affairs, so she visited other countries. While in the Soviet Union, she was called "the Iron Lady" by a newspaper. Margaret liked the name. She felt that her country could use an iron lady, so she adopted the nickname in her campaign to become leader of her party.

"The things [women] know are very different from what men know.... Any woman who understands the problems of running a home will be nearer to understanding the problems of running the country."

Margaret's training as a lawyer helped her when she made presentations to the House of Commons.

Accomplishments

In 1979, Margaret became the first woman prime minister of Great Britain and Northern Ireland. Although Margaret was not popular with everyone, she won the respect of many people. She worked to help business and reduce taxes. In 1982, she impressed people with her handling of the Falklands War between Britain and Argentina which Britain won.

Margaret was always a hard worker. She refused to give in to any kind of illness and rarely took time off. She managed to convince the country that the government had to reduce spending to improve Britain's economic situation. Margaret's work paid off, and she was re-elected in 1983.

In 1984, the Irish Republican Army (IRA) planted a bomb in Margaret's hotel room. The IRA was using terrorism to try to convince the British government to give up its control over Northern Ireland. The bomb went off in the middle of the night. Had Margaret been asleep, she might have been killed, but she was up writing a speech. Margaret stayed calm, and the next day she delivered her speech.

Although Margaret had a reputation for being a tough leader, many people found her down-to-earth and generous. British prime ministers and their staff have a Christmas tradition in which the staff invites the prime minister for a holiday dinner. Margaret changed the tradition by inviting the staff to her house where she served dinner herself.

Margaret was elected for a third time in 1987. In 1990, she stepped down as leader when some of her policies became unpopular with the public and members of her party. Since her retirement, Margaret has spoken out on international affairs and runs the Thatcher Foundation, an organization that helps businesses in Eastern Europe.

BACKGROUNDER

The Cold War

The Cold War was the struggle between **communist** and **democratic** nations that began after World War II. The war was "cold" because it never involved open fighting. During the 1980s, Margaret met many times with the leader of the Soviet Union, Mikhail Gorbachev, and the president of the United States, Ronald Reagan. They discussed reducing weapons and a possible end to the war. Margaret played an important part in ending the hostilities between the two countries.

In 1992, Queen Elizabeth II gave Margaret the title Baroness Thatcher of Kesteven. She is now known as Lady Thatcher and has the right to a seat in the House of Lords.

More Women in Profile

You have just read about some remarkable political leaders.
The following pages list a few you might want to learn about on your own. Use
the Suggested Reading list to learn more about these and other women leaders.

1916–

Sirimavo Bandaranaike
Prime Minister of Ceylon (Sri Lanka)

Only after her husband, the prime minister of Ceylon, was **assassinated** in 1959, did Sirimavo enter politics. In 1960, she was elected the world's first woman prime minister. Sirimavo was called Mrs. Banda by the Ceylonese people. She was prime minister until 1965 and then again from 1970 to 1977. Sirimavo worked hard to improve the role of women in her country. She was prime minister when Ceylon gained **independence** from Britain in 1972 and changed its name to Sri Lanka.

1939–

Gro Harlem Brundtland
Prime Minister of Norway

Gro, pronounced "grew," is a medical doctor who has been elected prime minister of Norway three times: 1981, 1986, and 1990. Gro supports women's rights and has always tried to have an equal number of men and women as members of her government. She is respected around the world for her work as head of a United Nations commission on the environment.

1929–

Violeta Chamorro
President of Nicaragua

Violeta entered politics when her husband was assassinated by the dictator of Nicaragua, Anastasio Samoza. She became publisher of her husband's newspaper, *La Pressa,* and continued his work against the **dictatorship**. In 1990, she was elected to a six-year term as president. She ended her country's long civil war and became a symbol of hope for the people of Nicaragua.

Violeta Chamorro

1919–

Eugenia Charles

Prime Minister of Dominica

"To me equality is the important thing. I don't want preferences.... But I want it acknowledged that I am a human being who has the capacity to do what I have to do, and it doesn't matter whether I was born a man or woman."

Eugenia studied law and economics. She became prime minister of Dominica in 1980. Eugenia worked to make her government honest. She increased her country's defense forces and made Dominica less dependent on help from other countries.

1947–

Hillary Rodham Clinton

First Lady of the United States

Hillary became nationally known when she helped her husband's campaign to become president of the United States. As first lady, she has tried to create a new national health care program and has supported programs for education and children.

1930–

Vigdis Finnbogadóttir

President of Iceland

"We all know that women have to do everything a little better than men.... We're all so very, very tolerant when men make mistakes, but I don't know of any society that is tolerant when women make mistakes."

Vigdis began her career by teaching French. She went on to work in the theater where she produced and directed plays. She also taught drama. Vigdis was elected president in 1980. Her most important job is to bring Iceland's culture to the rest of the world. She is popular among the people of Iceland who call her President Vigdis.

Hillary Rodham Clinton

1947–

Sheikh Hasina

Prime Minister of Bangladesh

Sheikh's father, Bangabandhu Sheikh Mujibur Rahman, is considered to be the Father of Bangladesh. Sheikh learned about politics while helping her father with his government duties. She was out of the country when he was **assassinated** in 1975. She could not return until 1981. In that year, she was elected president of her country's largest political party. She worked hard to end military control of the government. She was elected prime minister in 1996.

1941–

Maria Liberia-Peters

Prime Minister of the Netherlands Antilles

"We are not yet there, but it's very important that we see that more and more countries are appointing women as their political leaders, as prime ministers, as presidents, and I think that's a very important development."

Maria used to be a kindergarten teacher. She was prime minister of her Caribbean country from 1984 to 1986 and from 1988 to 1994. Maria was not a traditional prime minister. During a Carnival parade, instead of watching from the prime minister's viewing stand, she danced in the street with the crowd.

1943–

Ertha Pascal-Trouillot

President of Haiti

In a country where ninety percent of the population cannot read, Ertha managed not only to learn to read, but also to become a lawyer. She was the first woman in the Supreme Court of Haiti. She was president of Haiti from 1990 to 1991.

1931–

Isabel Perón

President of Argentina

Isabel was the third wife of Juan Perón, the president of Argentina. When he died in 1974, she took his place as president. Two years later, the military took over Argentina, removed Isabel from power, and sent her to Spain. In 1983, the military gave up power and allowed **elections**. Isabel returned to her country, but she did not go back to politics.

Isabel Perón

1943–

Kazimiera Prunskiene

Prime Minister of Lithuania

In 1990, Kazimiera was prime minister of Lithuania for ten months. This was a difficult time in her country's history. Lithuania was trying to separate from the Soviet Union (U.S.S.R.), so the U.S.S.R. refused to send oil, gas, or **raw materials** to Lithuania. Soon after Kazimiera resigned, the U.S.S.R. recognized Lithuania's **independence**.

Kazimiera Prunskiene

1944–

Mary Robinson

President of Ireland

Mary was president of Ireland from 1990 to 1997. She believes strongly in women's rights and the rights of people with physical and mental disabilities. She has worked to get equal pay for women and to make divorce and birth control legal in her country.

1884–1962

Eleanor Roosevelt

First Lady of the United States

Eleanor was married to Franklin Delano Roosevelt who was president of the United States from 1933 to 1945. Eleanor began to do political work for her husband when he became ill with polio in 1921. She became famous for her work with youth, low-income people, and minority groups. From 1945 to 1951, Eleanor was the United States representative to the United Nations General Assembly. She helped write the U.N. Universal Declaration of Human Rights.

Glossary

assassinate: to murder someone, especially a politically important person

bankrupt: without money, unable to pay debts

civil rights: the rights of a member of a country

communist: supporting communism —the belief that the state should control all property and methods of production

constitution: a document stating the laws of a country

corrupt: dishonest, taking money or bribes

debating: arguing reasons for and against a certain topic

democracy: a government in which people can elect their political leaders

dictatorship: a government in which one person rules a country with complete power

diplomacy: managing talks among countries

election: choosing a leader by voting

embalm: to treat a dead body with chemicals to keep it from decaying

hunger strike: refusing to eat until one's demands are granted

independence: freedom from control by another person or country

Islam: a religion that believes there is only one God, Allah, and follows the teachings of the prophet Mohammed

liaison: a person who goes between two or more groups trying to maintain contact or settle a dispute

morale: a feeling of courage and confidence

Muslim: a believer of Islam

persecute: to treat badly and oppress, especially for political, religious, or racial reasons

political party: a group of people who have the same political beliefs and want to form a government

raw materials: material that can or will be manufactured into something else

strategic: important, especially for war

surrender: to give up control of something

terrorize: to use violence to force a government or organization to support a particular cause

tolerance: willingness to understand another person's ideas or beliefs

United Nations: a world-wide organization that works for peace and equality

Suggested Reading

Currimbhoy, Nayana. *Indira Gandhi*. New York: Franklin Watts, 1985.

Faber, Doris. *Margaret Thatcher: Britain's "Iron Lady."* New York: Viking Kestrel, 1985.

Fishlock, Trevor. *Indira Gandhi*. London: Hamish Hamilton, 1986.

Hughes, Libby. *Benazir Bhutto: From Prison to Prime Minister.* Minneapolis: Dillon Press, Inc., 1990.

Keller, Mollie. *Golda Meir.* New York: Franklin Watts, 1983.

Liswood, Laura A. *Women World Leaders: Fifteen Great Politicians Tell Their Stories.* London: HarperCollins, 1995.

Opfell, Olga S. *Women Prime Ministers and Presidents.* Jefferson, North Carolina: McFarland & Company Inc, 1993.

Raven, Susan and Alison Weir. *Women of Achievement: Thirty-five Centuries of History.* New York: Harmony Books, 1981.

Royston, Angela. *100 Greatest Women.* London: Dragon's World Ltd., 1995.

Saari, Peggy. *Prominent Women of the 20th Century.* New York: UXL, 1996.

Seigel, Beatrice. *Cory: Corazon Aquino and the Philippines.* New York: E.P. Dutton, 1988.

Taylor, J. M. *Evita Perón: The Myths of a Woman.* Oxford: Basil Blackwell, 1979.

Index

1 2 3 4 5 6 7 8 9 0 Printed in Canada 7 6 5 4 3 2 1 0 9 8